Looking at Stars

Stars and Galaxies

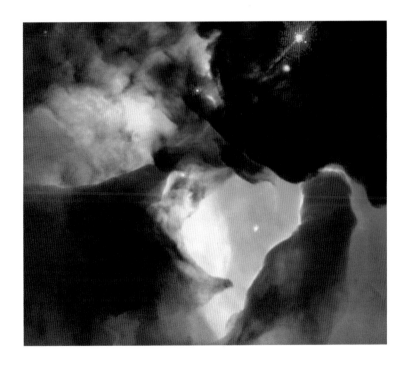

Robin Kerrod

Belitha Press

First published in the UK in 2001 by
Belitha Press Limited, London House,
Great Eastern Wharf, Parkgate Road,
London SW11 4NQ

ISBN 1 84138 329 5

British Library Cataloguing in Publication Data
for this book is available from the British Library.

Printed in Hong Kong

10 9 8 7 6 5 4 3 2 1

Editor: Veronica Ross
Designer: Helen James
Illustrator: Chris Forsey
Consultant: Doug Millard
Picture researcher: Diana Morris

Picture credits
Anglo-Australian Telescope/Robin Kerrod: 23t. © The Association of Universities for
Research in Astronomy, Inc/Spacecharts: 6b. K Borne (ST Scl)/ NASA/Spacecharts: 27t.
R Elson & R Sword (Cambridge University) and NASA/Spacecharts: 13t.
Robin Kerrod: 6-7, 7t, 8bl, 25t. Kitt Peak Observatory/Spacecharts: 4-5.
NASA/Spacecharts: 9t, 28t. Spacecharts: front cover c, 1, 5c, 8cr, 9cr, 10b, 11t,
15t, 16c, 17t, 17b, 18bl, 18br, 19t, 19c, 20b, 23b, 26b, 27b, 28c, 29c.
R Williams (ST Scl) NASA/Spacecharts: 29b.

Whilst every attempt has been made to clear copyrights should there
be inadvertent omissions please apply to the publisher for rectification.

Contents

Introducing stars and galaxies

The sky at night is a beautiful sight, full of thousands of twinkling **stars**. People have gazed up at the stars for thousands of years. Studying the stars is a science called astronomy.

What are stars, those tiny pinpricks of light in the dark night sky? **Astronomers** tell us they are huge balls of very hot gas, like our Sun. They look tiny only because they are very far away in the inky blackness of space. Stars are distant suns.

Astronomers know a lot about the stars and how they are born, live and die. They tell of stars of many colours, of dwarf stars and giants, of stars that cluster together, and of stars that explode.

The stars are not scattered about throughout space. They gather together in huge groups, with empty space in between. They form great star islands, or **galaxies**. All the galaxies and the space between them make up the **Universe**.

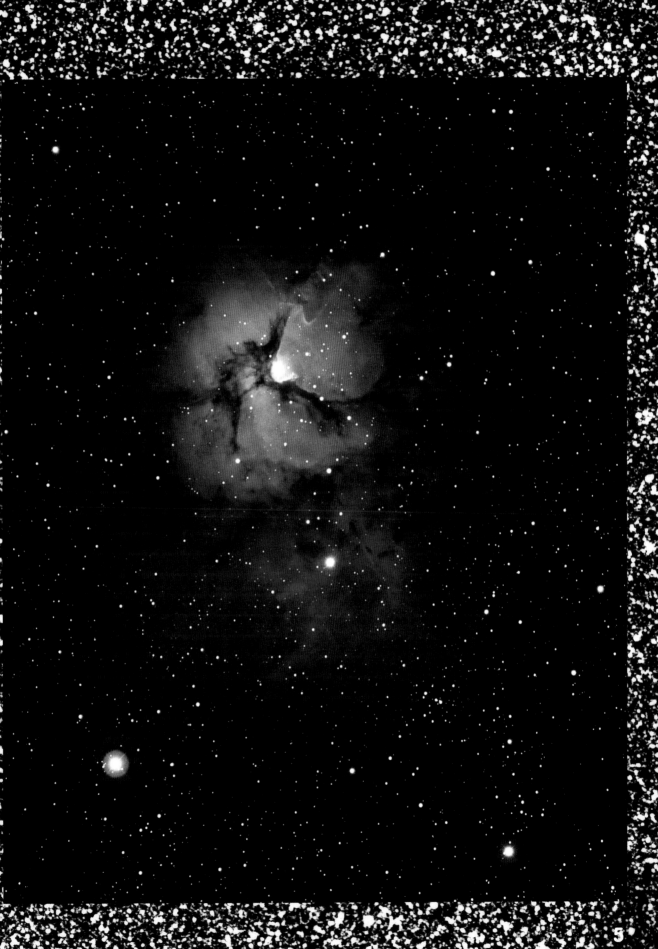

Studying stars

We can learn something about the **stars** using just our eyes. But we can find out a lot more when we use a **telescope**. Telescopes gather much more light than our eyes and make the stars look brighter and clearer. They can spot stars that are too faint for our eyes to see. Some telescopes use curved mirrors to gather light and focus it – make it form a sharp image (picture). We call these telescopes reflectors, because mirrors reflect light.

Other telescopes use lenses (curved pieces of glass) to gather and focus starlight. We call them refractors, because lenses refract (bend) light.

◁ **Big mirror**
This telescope collects light from the stars with a mirror four metres across.

Astronomers work at **observatories**, where their telescopes are housed in buildings with domes. The domes open at night to let the telescopes see the sky.

△ Using lenses

Many amateur astronomers use a refractor, or lens telescope, like this.

▷ Above the clouds

The telescopes at Kitt Peak Observatory, USA, stand on a mountain above the clouds. High up, the air is clearer and cleaner.

On the radio

We see the stars because our eyes can detect the light waves (rays) they give off. But stars also give off waves that our eyes can't see, such as radio waves.

Astronomers use special radio telescopes to pick up radio waves from space. Most radio telescopes have huge metal dishes, which act as aerials to pick up the waves.

▽ Tuning in

The Parkes radio telescope in Australia gathers radio waves from stars and galaxies.

△ Radio pictures

This picture of a galaxy has been taken using the radio waves it gives out.

▽ Star birth
The Hubble telescope spots vast clouds of gas, in which stars are being born and shining brightly for the first time.

△ Hubble telescope
The Hubble Space Telescope has been sending back amazing pictures since 1990.

Computers are used to change the pattern of radio waves coming from space into pictures. These radio pictures are quite different from ordinary light pictures.

Astronomers launch telescopes into space, which send back their pictures by radio. Space telescopes get a clearer view of the stars because they circle above Earth's dirty atmosphere.

Light-years away

Stars are distant suns. But just how far away are they? Let's see.

December and January are good times of the year to see the brightest star in the night sky, Sirius. Sirius is one of the nearest stars to us. But astronomers tell us it is nearly 90 million million (90 000 000 000 000) kilometres away! No one can imagine how far this is. So astronomers look at this distance another way.

◁ Hot stuff

*The brightest star we see here is called Capella. Its light takes nearly 50 years to reach us. We say it lies 50 **light-years** away.*

Astronomers know that the light from Sirius takes nearly 9 years to reach the Earth. So they say that the star is nearly 9 light-years away. 9 light-years is simpler than 90 000 000 000 000 kilometres!

◁ Speedy starship
To visit the distant stars, we would need to ride in a spaceship that travelled at fantastic speeds. This one has photon drive – it is powered by light beams.

Blazing suns

Like the Sun, stars are great glowing balls of very hot gas. They give out fantastic amounts of energy as light and heat.

From Earth, we can see that some stars look bright and others look dim. Astronomers measure the brightness of a star by its **magnitude**. First magnitude stars are the brightest.

Brightest of all is Sirius, also called the Dog Star because it is found in the **constellation** (star group) called the Great Dog.

▷ **A look inside**

If we could cut open a star, it might look like this. In the core (centre), it gobbles up atoms to produce energy. The energy rises to the surface and pours into space as light and heat.

▷ **Sparkling like jewels**
Colourful stars flash and sparkle like precious jewels. Their colour depends on how hot they are.

◁ **Daytime star**
Our local star, the Sun, gives out a yellowish light during the day. In the evening, it takes on an orange glow.

Stars in colour

Stars not only have different brightnesses, they also have different colours. The colours tell us how hot the stars are. The hottest stars are bluish-white. The coolest stars are reddish-orange. Medium-hot stars are yellowish. The Sun is a medium-hot star.

Dwarfs and giants

All the stars are different in size. Many stars are about the same size as our Sun. The Sun measures about 1 400 000 kilometres across, or over 100 times the size of the Earth. Some stars are much bigger than the Sun. So astronomers call the Sun a dwarf star.

Bigger stars are called giants, and the biggest stars of all are **supergiants**. Supergiants can be hundreds of times bigger across than the Sun. The reddish star Betelgeuse is one of the biggest supergiants. It is found in the **constellation** Orion.

Blue giant
Tens of times
bigger than Sun

▽ **Little** and **large**
Stars come in all sizes,
from tiny dwarfs to
gigantic supergiants.

Red giant
Tens of times
bigger than Sun

Supergiant
Hundreds of times
bigger than Sun

▷ Gas blast

A huge star called Eta Carinae blasts out a great cloud of gas and dust. Astronomers think that this star will soon blow itself to pieces.

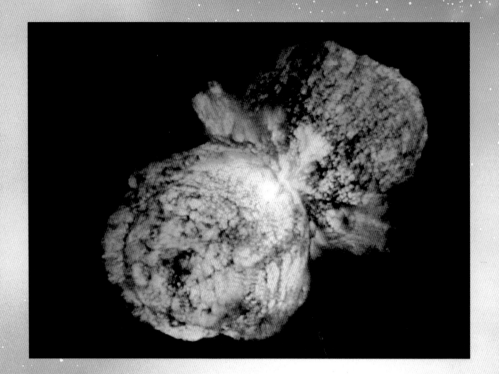

Heavyweights

There are other stars that are much smaller than the Sun. Many white dwarf stars are about as big as the Earth. Stars called **pulsars** are only about 20 kilometres across – smaller than some of our cities!

Pulsars are very, very heavy for their size. Just a teaspoonful of matter from a pulsar would weigh millions of tonnes!

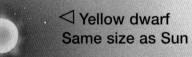

◁ Yellow dwarf
Same size as Sun

Getting together

The bright stars seem to form patterns in the night sky. These patterns always stay the same and help us find our way about the sky. We call them the constellations. The stars in a constellation appear to be grouped together in space. But they are not. In fact the stars lie different distances away. We see them together only because they just happen to lie in the same direction in space.

◁ Heavenly twins

The star constellation we call Gemini, meaning the Twins. The two bright stars marking the heads of the boys are named Castor and Pollux.

Clustering together

But some stars do group together in space to form star **clusters**. One famous cluster is the Pleiades. It is also called the Seven Sisters because some people can spot its seven bright stars with the naked eye. In fact, the cluster contains as many as 300 stars.

△ Seven Sisters

This is the cluster we call the Pleiades, or Seven Sisters. Its stars are young and hot.

Globes of stars

In some parts of the heavens, thousands upon thousands of stars are found grouped together. They form great balls, or globes, of stars and are known as globular clusters.

◁ **Great globe**

Hundreds of thousands of stars gather together to form this great globular cluster.

Heavenly clouds

When we look at the night sky, we see the stars and dark space in between. This space is almost empty – but not quite. It contains minute amounts of gas and tiny specks of dust. Here and there, the gas and dust gather together to form thick clouds, called **nebulas**. Some nebulas are found near stars. And they reflect (send back) the light from these stars. Then we see them lit up in bright colours.

Other nebulas are not near stars, and they are not lit up. We can see them only when they form dark patches against a bright background.

▽ **The Lagoon**
Astronomers call this glowing gas cloud the Lagoon Nebula.

▽ **The Rosette**
The wisps of red gas in the Rosette Nebula look like rose petals.

◁ **The Great Nebula**
We can see the Great Nebula with the naked eye in the constellation Orion.

▽ **Dark and bright**
The dark parts of this nebula show where there are clouds of dark gas.

Heavenly smoke

The main substance found in nebulas is hydrogen. This is also the main gas found in stars. Most of the dust in nebulas is carbon. You can think of a dusty nebula as heavenly smoke. The smoke garden bonfires give off is made up of specks of carbon.

Many other substances are found in nebulas. There is water and oxygen, the gas in Earth's air that keeps us alive. There are even carbon compounds like those found in our bodies.

Life stories

Night after night and year after year, the same stars appear in the sky. They don't seem to change at all. But the sky and the stars are changing – very slowly.

In many millions of years time, the sky will look quite different. Most of the stars we see today will have vanished. And new stars will have appeared. The stars we see now will have died and faded away. New stars will have been born and started to shine.

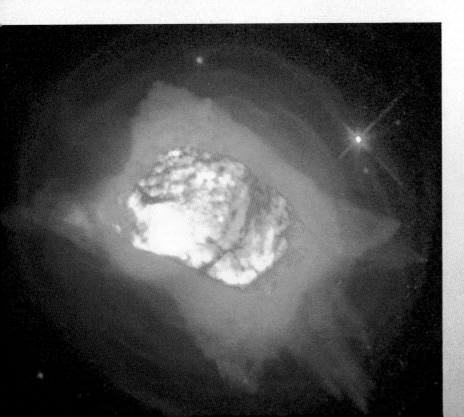

△ **Birthplace**
A cloud of gas and dust

△ **Long life**
All stars are born in great gas clouds. In time, stars like the Sun swell up into red giants. Then they shrink and end their lives as tiny white dwarfs.

◁ **Last gasp**
Inside this beautiful gas cloud is a dying star. Stars puff off gas many times as they die.

▽ Shining star
The hot ball becomes
a star and starts to
shine steadily

▽ Swelling up
In old age the star
swells up, getting
bigger and bigger

△ Shrinking ball
A mass of gas
shrinks into a ball
shape and heats up

Star birth

Stars are born in great clouds
of gas and dust, called nebulas.
From time to time, a thick part
of a nebula becomes even
thicker. This happens when
the gas and dust particles
(bits) start to pull each other.
This pull is called **gravity**.

Gravity makes the thick cloud
shrink into a small ball. The ball
becomes hotter and hotter. In
time, it starts to shine as a star.

The star shines for millions of
years, but then it starts to die.
A star like the Sun swells up
into a giant, then shrinks
to a tiny dwarf.

▷ Red giant
The star turns
redder and
becomes
giant sized

▷ Shrinking giant
In time the giant
star shrinks

△ Puffing gas
As the star
shrinks, it
puffs off gas

△ White dwarf
The star ends up as
a tiny, hot white dwarf

Out with a bang

Stars about the same size as the Sun live for a long time. They shine for thousands of millions of years before they swell up and start to die.

Heavier stars have much shorter lives. Some shine for only a few million years before they start to die. And they swell up to a much greater size than lighter stars. They become great supergiants, hundreds of times bigger than the Sun.

Super bangs

Heavy stars do not stay supergiants for long. Soon they explode and blast themselves to pieces. For a while, they become millions of times brighter and shine like beacons in space. Exploding stars are called **supernovas**.

Red giant

Supergiant
The giant star
swells up into
a supergiant

▷ Supernova!
When a very big star dies, it grows into an enormous supergiant. Then it explodes as a supernova.

◁ Heavenly beacon
A supernova lights up the heavens like a beacon in February 1987.

▽ Strange circles
Today, circles of glowing gas are found where the 1987 supernova blew up.

Lighthouse stars

Most of an exploding star is blasted into space. Only a tiny, very heavy ball of matter is left. It is about the size of a city.

The ball spins round and sends out beams of light. If the beams reach Earth, we see them as flashes, or pulses. This is why we call these bodies pulsars.

Black holes

A very big star shrinks to almost nothing and becomes a **black hole** in space. In a black hole, gravity is very strong. It even holds back light rays. This is why we can never see a black hole.

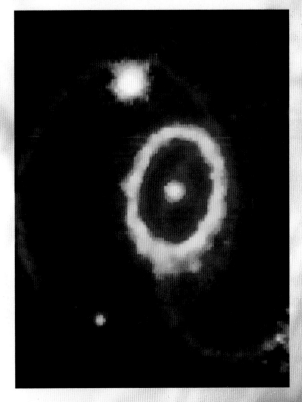

Our star island

The night sky is full of stars. They seem to be scattered about everywhere in space. But they are not.

If you could travel in a starship far out into space, you would in time leave the stars behind. When you looked back, you would see the stars grouped together into a great star island. If you looked around, you would see in the distance other star islands, surrounded by a black sea of space. These star islands in space are called galaxies.

▷ **Curving arms**

This is what our galaxy might look like if we could see it from afar. The stars sit on arms that curve out from the centre.

24

The Milky Way

We call our galaxy the Milky Way. It is shaped like a disc, with a bulge in the middle. Altogether, it contains about 100 000 million stars. Most stars sit on arms that curve out of the bulge.

The whole galaxy turns round slowly. From a distance, it would look like a spinning Catherine Wheel firework.

△ Milky Way
In the night sky, we see a thick part of our galaxy as a milk-white band. We call this the Milky Way.

25

Galaxies galore

There are millions of other galaxies in space. Many of them look like our own galaxy. They are shaped like a disc with a bulge in the middle. And their stars sit on curved arms. We call these kinds of galaxies spirals.

Other galaxies have round or oval shapes and are called ellipticals. Others have no particular shape at all, and are called irregulars.

We can see a few of the nearest galaxies with the naked eye. We can see one in the Northern Hemisphere (northern half) of the world in the constellation Andromeda. It is a spiral.

We can see two more in the Southern Hemisphere. They are called the Large and Small Magellanic Clouds. They are irregulars.

◁ Neighbour
The Andromeda galaxy is one of the closest galaxies to us.

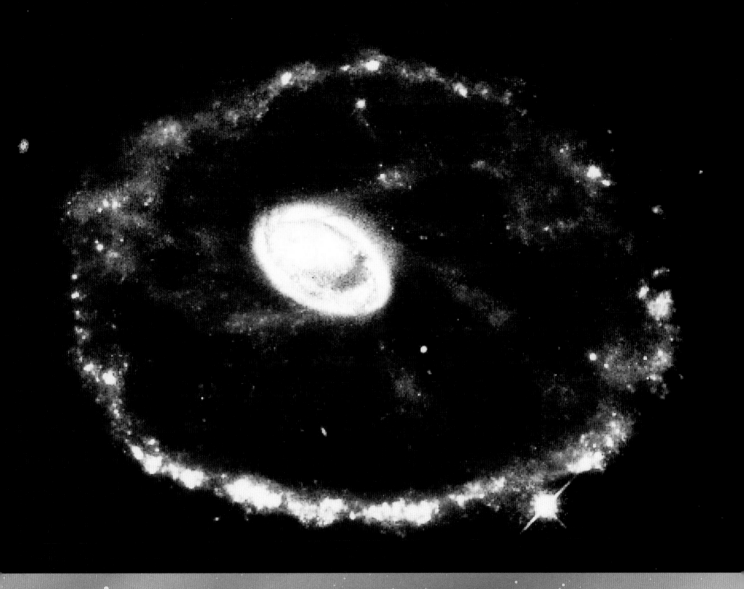

△ Colliding galaxies

The Cartwheel galaxy was formed when two galaxies collided millions of years ago.

▷ The Whirlpool

This famous galaxy is known as the Whirlpool because of its shape.

◁ **The Earth**
Earth is a planet.

▽ **The Sun**
Planets circle the Sun.

The great Universe

Through their telescopes, astronomers can see millions of galaxies in all directions in space. Galaxies and space make up what we call the **Universe**.

To us, the Earth we live on is the most important thing there is. But in the vast Universe, the Earth is very unimportant. It is like a tiny grain of sand in a vast ocean of space.

The galaxies are not scattered about evenly in space. They gather together into groups, or clusters. Our galaxy is part of a cluster of about 30 galaxies. But some clusters contain several thousand galaxies. In their turn, clusters of galaxies gather together into even larger groups, called superclusters. Many of these superclusters make up the Universe.

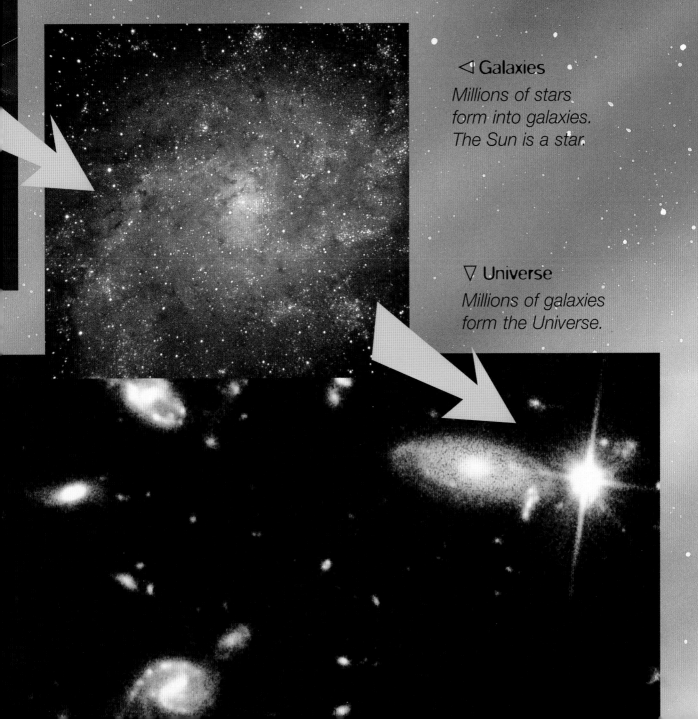

◁ Galaxies
Millions of stars form into galaxies. The Sun is a star.

▽ Universe
Millions of galaxies form the Universe.

The Big Bang

Astronomers find that the galaxies are racing away from one another. It seems as if the whole Universe is expanding (getting bigger). If the Universe is expanding, this means that it must have been smaller in the past. Once it must have been very small. Astronomers think this was 15 000 million years ago.

They think that the Universe was born about this time in a great explosion they call the Big Bang. This explosion set the Universe expanding until it became like it is today.

The Universe expands

Big Bang

Astronomers are not sure what will happen to the Universe. Maybe it will go on expanding. Or maybe it will start to shrink, and all its matter squash together in a Big Crunch.

Useful words

astronomer A person who studies the stars and all the other heavenly bodies.

black hole A region of space that has very strong gravity.

cluster A close group of stars.

constellation A pattern of bright stars.

galaxy A great star island in space, containing billions of stars.

gravity The pull every lump of matter has on every other lump.

light-year The distance light travels in a year, about 10 million million kilometres.

magnitude The brightness of a star.

nebula A huge cloud of gas and dust.

observatory A place where astronomers look at the stars.

pulsar A tiny spinning star that gives off beams, or pulses, of energy.

star A huge ball of very hot gases, which pours out energy into space.

supergiant The biggest kind of star.

supernova An exploding star.

telescope An instrument used to study the stars.

Universe Everything that exists – stars, planets, moons and space.

Index